This book is dedicated to the memory of Sandy Alewine and Marcus Smucker who served me as spiritual directors and mentors.

~ Dr. Eldon Fry

This book is dedicated to Eden Leigh Fry, whose path never developed, the daughter I was never able to get to know.

~ Marc Fry

Sacred
PATHWAY

DEVOTIONS AND REFLECTIONS
BY A FATHER AND SON

ELDON E. FRY
AND MARC A. FRY

WESTBOW
PRESS®
A DIVISION OF THOMAS NELSON
& ZONDERVAN

WestBow Press books may be ordered through booksellers or by contacting:

WestBow Press
A Division of Thomas Nelson & Zondervan
1663 Liberty Drive
Bloomington, IN 47403
www.westbowpress.com
844-714-3454

Scripture quotations are taken from the Holy Bible, NEW INTERNATIONAL VERSION®, NIV® Copyright © 1973, 1978, 1984, 2011 by Biblica, Inc.® Used by permission. All rights reserved worldwide.

Scriptures quotations are taken from the Holy Bible, New Living Translation, copyright © 1996, 2004, 2015 by Tyndale House Foundation. Used by permission of Tyndale House Publishers Inc., Carol Stream, Illinois 60188. All rights reserved.

ISBN: 979-8-3850-2040-9 (sc)
ISBN: 979-8-3850-2041-6 (e)

Library of Congress Control Number: 2024904458

Print information available on the last page.

WestBow Press rev. date: 12/17/2024

Contents

Introduction

EARLY CHRISTIANS WERE REFERRED TO AS "PEOPLE OF THE
Way". Greek nomenclature *"hodos" means a road or a path,
a travelled road or path and by implication a journey. In John
14:5,6 (NIV), Jesus declares* in response to Thomas statement
and question, *"Lord, we don't know where you are going, so how
can we know the way?" Jesus replies "I am the way and the truth
and the life."*

According to Acts 9:1,2 (NIV) Saul, a zealous pharisee,
was *"uttering threats with every breath and was eager to kill the
Lord's followers. So ...he requested letters from the high priest
to the synagogues in Damascus asking for their cooperation in
the arrest of followers of the Way he found there."* Belonging to
"the Way" meant suffering and persecution and perhaps death.
Little wonder that Jesus said Mark 8:34 (NIV) *"If anyone would
come after me, he must deny himself and take up his cross and
follow me."* Paul before the governor Felix admitted in Acts
24 that he had indeed become a follower of Jesus, a *"follower
of the Way"* (:14 NIV) In a world still clamoring for us follow
different paths, apparently the pathway we choose to follow will
determine our destination.

Eldon's birthdate in 1946 means that I was born during the
first year attributed to the Boomer generation. My son Marc
was born in 1970, growing up in the 70s and 80s. Eldon was

born in the mountain culture of Idaho but Marc was born in the culture of the Midwest and has lived in multiple cities throughout the U.S. Marc and I experienced life from different contexts, friendships and cultural experiences. His education and mine are different, yet we have embraced the Way in our unique understandings of what it means to follow Jesus. Even though we both have experienced distinct life experiences, we are both followers of the Way but see the path through the lens of our generations and cultural influences and experiences. We welcome you to read the chapters noting how our expressions and chapters may differ in style and focus but hopefully they help you to embrace your understanding and commitment to join us on the pathway of a life following Jesus.

Marc is the author of *The Struggle*(available on Amazon) and Eldon is the author of *Growing Up Idaho and Spiritual Formation: Attention Along the Way* (both available on Amazon). Marc and I have enjoyed watching and playing sports throughout our lives. Marc has pursued playing and coaching at higher levels in his life. We are family but very different people who thought we would have fun writing together in different styles about the Pathway.

Faith

(by Marc Fry)

"FAITH IS THE ASSURANCE OF THINGS HOPED FOR, THE conviction of things not seen (Hebrews 11:1)." What do we believe? What do we hope for? Both of these questions are rooted in faith. Our beliefs and morals are not always tangible things we can reach out and touch. The things we hope for are based on the future and have not yet come into occurrence.

Chapter 11 in Hebrews puts faith into tangible events for us. It starts with the creation and continues to recount all the things that occurred to help us have the confidence we need to believe that God is real and upholds his promises. Abel, Enoch, Noah, Abraham, Isaac, Jacob, Joseph, Moses, Rahab (the prostitute), Gideon and David are all mentioned in this chapter as people who had incredible faith.

Each of the people mentioned lived incredible lives of faith. God used them in amazing ways because he could rely on them because of their faith. The writer of Hebrews tells us, "And without faith it is impossible to please God, for he who comes to God must believe that He exists, and He is a rewarder of those who diligently seek Him (Hebrews 11:6)."

Isn't this what religion is based on? Believing there is a God, believing He is involved in our lives, believing there is power through Him, and believing that we were created for a purpose? Christianity takes it a step further, there is belief in Jesus Christ, the Son of God, who came to earth to live with, encourage and ultimately sacrifice his life for all persons. However, that is not the end. Jesus Christ overcame death so we might have life and have a direct relationship with God. If we choose to believe this, and have faith in Jesus, death has no power over us anymore.

Sometimes our minds just can't comprehend the events in the Bible, or how God is involved in current situations. Doubt is often used by the enemy to make us question reality and who God is. When I struggle with doubt, I take time to recount everything God has done in my life. Remembering all the things that have happened, both good and bad. I thank him for the good and trust him that he will redeem the losses and struggles we've had. Memorizing scripture is imperative to build a person's faith. God will not turn away from his promises.

Here are some verses to memorize if you are a Child of God:

- James 4:10
- Galatians 5:16
- Psalm 34:18
- Deuteronomy 31:6
- 2 Timothy 1:7

One of God's promises to those who believe in him is that "All things work for good to those who love God and live according to his purpose (Romans 8:28)." That is an incredible verse. It is very difficult to comprehend. God has a purpose and a plan, but he also gives us free will to choose or reject his plan and purpose for our lives. The world is full of evil and brokenness. Terrible things happen to people. I will never understand fully as to why people experience so much pain and loss. I do however believe what Romans 8:28 tells us. God will redeem all things to those who believe in him and live according to his purpose.

Redemption has no timeline. Redemption can be a process of steps, or it can be instantaneously. Redemption requires Faith. Jesus Christ is known as the Redeemer. One day, perhaps not until his return for some, those who believe and have faith will experience full redemption. It tells us in Isaiah that God will make things new. "See, I will do a new thing, now it shall spring forth; shall you not be aware of it? I will even make a way in the wilderness, and rivers in the desert (Isaiah 43:19)."

In the end, what do we really have besides our faith? One of the disciples responded to Jesus by saying, "To whom else would we go?" How deep is your faith? Have you allowed God into your life to experience redemption? Strengthen your faith by reading, memorizing scripture and communicating with God.

Read Hebrews 11

Transition, Trauma and Truth

(by Eldon Fry)

LIFE HAS CHANGED FOR ME. SOME DAYS I AM GASPING FOR AIR to catch up with this new era in my life. My wife has been diagnosed with Alzheimer's and I have moved my office home to be a better caretaker with the help of our children and grandchildren. I am being treated for back pain that has limited my own activity. Life now has smaller parameters. I need to plan grocery trips and doctor visits and stay home in evenings to attend to my wife and no longer participate in evening events or appointments. My body and mind feel the change and struggle to adjust to my new reality. But I know I am not alone in facing change. Change is essential for life and a common topic in the conversations I have with other friends and clients through Open Hands.

Rapid change is sweeping America like an unexpected tsunami. Sociologists research it and authors like Len Sweet (Rings of Fire) describe it as walking in faith through a volcanic future. Constant and rapid change takes a toll on my soul. Research affirms that we are searching for something stabilizing in the drama of uncertainties. We live in a culture with multiple disruptions in our everyday lives. It feels like dramatic change is in the very air we breathe. We are still processing the results of a season of unlimited internet availability and cultural pressure to be relevant and current even viral using this tool. Our minds are now opened to unlimited access to social media, the revamping of ethical values and morals, a global pandemic has touched every family and friendship circle, a loss of trust in our institutions and common history, racial, genetic and gender divisions and political divisiveness. How do we, can we reorient and discover stability to these new realities? How can we breathe deeply?

While life only survives and expands through transitions and change. How do we find new hope in a world that seemingly is upside down and chaotic? The Psalmist lived in an age of external aggression, internal divisiveness and unsettling political maneuvering but was inspired to pen these ancient words to those delighting in God's words, "They are like trees planted along the riverbank, bearing fruit each season. (Psalm 1:2,3 NLT) and later he affirmed "...for the Lord watches over the path of the godly." (Psalm 1:6 NLT) What an idyllic perspective. Our family lives close to a stream where trees grow tall and beautiful. However, they also come crashing down and have caused many electrical outages because of their falling. We adjusted by purchasing a generator to keep the electrical service rather groping around in darkness.

Autumn colors are descending outside, and change is in the coolness of the morning breeze. Birds gather in flocks for a journey south to warmer climes. As trees let go of their colorful leaves, they create a patchwork quilt on the dry ground. The season reminds us that underneath the leafy quilt, life is already birthing another season of fruit and crops to harvest and green grass to mow next summer. Change is necessary but our souls long for stability, a rootedness to survive the winds of the tsunami of change.

How did Abram survive the call of God to a new land (Genesis 12) when the language indicates it was a journey with a lot of questions, uncertainties, and dangers? Although Abram was on a journey, he was solidly rooted in the values and call of his God. Somehow that rootedness would be the basis for Jews, Muslims and Christians to refer to him as "Father Abraham." The truth of the gospel is stable but adaptable to changing times. John declares, "I have written to you who are God's children because you know the Father. I have written to you who are mature in the faith because you know Christ, who existed from the beginning. I have written to you who are young in faith because you are strong. God's word lives in your hearts and you have won your battle with the evil one." (I John 2:14 NLT). As we encounter change, chaos, or trouble, we experience shifts in context and culture which can produce trauma but knowing there is a certain center we remain grounded and filled with hope as expressed by the beloved disciple, John and the apostle, Paul. "So, we don't look at the troubles we can see now; rather we fix our gaze on things that cannot be seen. For the things we see now will soon be gone, but the things we cannot see will last forever." (II Corinthians 4:18 NLT)

Yes, transitions, trauma and changes are a part of the reality of our lives. But the one who said, "I am the way the truth, and the life." (John 14:6 NLT) Is the one who stated he would never leave us or forsake us. The psalmist, poet says, "Even when I walk through the darkest valley, I will not be afraid for you are close beside me."

Today's event was another journey to our family doctor's office to receive the recommended flu shot for people our age. It was a small sample of the cataclysmic changes in the parameters of our lives. But my wife and I can laugh about my forgetfulness, and we can still enjoy lunch together and returning home to watch several minutes of a western while snuggling on our love seat. We do that with faith as the center in our lives built around truth that will sustain through the storms forecasted for our lives.

Q. What are the roots of faith that gives your life stability in seasonal changes?

The Sabbath

(by Marc Fry)

MOST OF US KNOW THE SABBATH AS SUNDAY, OR A DAY A person may or may not go to church. The Sabbath was the 7th day when God rested after completing the Creation. The 10 Commandments state to "Remember the Sabbath and keep it Holy." The Sabbath was sacred. Our God is holy and demands holiness. Jews were required to follow the laws placed upon them for the Sabbath, but the laws often went too far and went beyond what God had intended. There was to be no work done on the Sabbath. Traditional Jewish rules for the Sabbath included the following:

- The Law of Bread: planting, plowing, gathering sorting, grinding, and cooking (all prohibited).
- The Order of Garments: sewing, dyeing, laundering, combing, and weaving (all prohibited).
- The Order of Hides: trapping, killing, skinning, treating, and smoothing (all prohibited).
- The Order of Construction: transporting, building, demolition, fires, and writing (all prohibited).
  www.theisraelbible.com

One of the few things that **was allowed** was the teaching and studying of the scriptures on the Sabbath. Jesus would often be found on the Sabbath in the synagogue teaching and listening to others. Religious leaders would often gather for study, prayer and conversation. While Jesus was in the synagogue, he saw a woman who had a physical impairment or disability. The Bible tells us she had been bent over for 18 years and was unable to stand up straight. When Jesus saw the woman he said, "Woman you are loosed from your infirmity." After saying this he laid his hands on her and immediately she was able to stand straight. The woman, being healed from her iniquity, began to praise God.

It was then that a religious leader of the synagogue told the crowd that there were 6 days to work during the week and if someone were to seek healing, it should be done then and not on the Sabbath. Jesus responded by calling him a **_HYPOCRITE!_** He said, "You move your donkeys and your ox for water, shouldn't this woman, a daughter of Abraham, be loosed from bondage on the Sabbath?" Others began to rejoice for the miracles Jesus had done, but the leaders had been humiliated in front of the crowd.

In Luke 6 we are told there was a man with a withered hand. It must have been curled up and unable to move, or perhaps it was deteriorating from a disease. Jesus was once again in the synagogue this Sabbath day. The religious leaders hovered around to see if Jesus would heal on the Sabbath, then they could accuse him of wrongdoing. The passage states that Jesus knew their thoughts. He addressed the man with the withered hand and had him stand up in front of everyone. Jesus then said to the crowd, "I will ask you one thing: Is it lawful on the Sabbath to do good or evil, to save a life or destroy it?" He then looked around and said to the man, "Stretch out your hand." Instantly his hand was healed. Madness occurred and the leaders began to plot about what they might do to Jesus.

Jesus was rebellious on the Sabbath in a righteous way. He was tired of the hypocrisy and all the legalism that the Sabbath had turned into. He called out the religious leaders who scrutinized everyone but themselves. His intent for the Sabbath was for followers to worship God and to remember what he had done for them. Jesus loved people and desired good. What kind of God would he have been if he had not healed on the Sabbath, the day that was designated for himself?

I find it interesting that despite the legalism, Jesus still went to the Synagogue. He desired to be around the scriptures and others who wanted to learn and even healed. What if the two persons with ailments had not gone to the synagogue? I'm sure they had experienced rejection at some point by religious leaders because of their disabilities. It couldn't have been easy for them to enter through the doors into the place of worship. How often have we experienced rejection from the church because we don't have things quite right, know the right person, or the right etiquette?

The church was intended to be a place for discipleship, forgiveness, healing, learning and encouragement. It's not a place for rejection. Jesus refuted the religious zealots because he had the integrity, knowledge, and authority to do so. He valued helping others more than following legalistic laws. How often have we turned others away from worship and healing because of our own actions?

These questions also need to be asked. Do we even keep the Sabbath anymore? The death and resurrection of Jesus has freed us from the legalism of the past, but do we take time to worship? Do we take time to respect and recognize God with others? Do we step away from work, athletics and running around all over the place to slow down and acknowledge God? Do we step away from the sins, burdens, and heaviness of this world to seek healing in our own lives?

Let us be encouraged to take time to worship the Lord with others, seek healing in our lives, seek forgiveness of our faults, and to be thankful to the Lord for all he has done for us and brought us through. Let us do this not only once a week but let us do it daily as we walk on the path with Jesus. Let us make the Sabbath a part of our lives.

Read Luke 6:6-11 and Luke 13:10-17

The Path not Taken (Choices)

(by Eldon Fry)

CURRENT CHOICES HAVE LED ME TO FEEL LIKE I HAVE TURNED off a major highway and traveled on sideroads, ending up on a dead-end gravel road. I can still get where I am going but eventually it will narrow to the point that I can go no further. I used to quote Robert Frost's popular poem, The Road not Taken, and assumed my decisions in the morning *"...both equally lay in leaves no step had trodden."* There was a certain excitement to be a pioneer of sorts on an unmarked path. The options seemed limitless as I explored new territory and blazed new paths but aging, the great equalizer, slowly gave me pause, *"with a sigh"* and led me to evaluate what if I had chosen another path. What if I had traveled down a more common road and not taken the risks of unchartered territory?

Aging is a time that creates space for reflection. "What ifs" can circle my mind like vultures waiting for a tragic death in a wilderness, alone and unprepared. Yet somehow from deep within there is a voice or more a sense that the choice was meant to be. Choices by their very nature demand a decision which is birthed in "either-or" and sometimes the evaluations of the past are painful but typically not fatal. I assumed that I would face less choices at this age but each day with a wife who has

Alzheimers is like choosing a new path wherever the fog parts for a few minutes.

The backroads of Pennsylvania often are covered with fog on autumn mornings contained in the valleys where the streams raise moisture into the sky blocking the visual of the roadway ahead. It is dangerous to drive through the fog but life keeps moving ahead and decisions are made and secured by time. Should we move or not, should we change doctors, are there new medications that could be helpful, what about all the ads on social media that claim answers hidden by big pharma, what about stepping back from obvious ministry to care for my wife, what helps her engage in life or irritates her with the realization of loss of her acuity? Fog and more fog. Am I the best caretaker for her, what does she really need and what is sustainable? Fog is real and I can look back and see those moments where we made lifetime decisions without seeing the implications and results of the path chosen. But I can only muse about the path not taken the choice not made. I pray that in the age to come my children and grandchildren will look upon those choices with grace and love and appreciate that we did the best we could with the insights and resources we had available to us at that moment when the choice had to be made.

Yet, there lingers an awareness of a path not taken and swirling thoughts of what could have been if another choice had been made. Even with that awareness knocking at the door of my brain, I can rest in peace because I chose to take the path of my choices and that has *made all the difference.*

Q. What is the "fog" that obscures the decision making in your. Life? How does trust in a "God who sees" help you have confidence in those choices you must make?

The 10 Lepers

(by Marc Fry)

I FIND THIS STORY FASCINATING. AS JESUS WAS WALKING FROM Samaria to Galilee, he entered a village and encountered 10 Lepers who were standing at a distance because of their disease. The Lepers cried out to him begging for mercy from their strife. Lepers were outcasts and were often isolated from others because of the disease. Jesus, having seen their strife and disease, told them to go see the priests. During those times, it was the priests who were responsible for the declaration of cleanliness of disease. As the Lepers went to seek out the priests, they were healed from their disease.

One of the 10 Lepers, realizing he had been healed, returned to Jesus praising God (with a loud voice) for what happened to him. His life had changed from death, disease and social rejection to healing, cleansing and restoration. Can you even imagine experiencing something so incredible?

When he returned, Jesus noticed the others were not with him. Jesus asked the man, "Where are the nine? Were there not 10 healed?" The man fell to the feet of Jesus and gave him thanks. Jesus looked at him and said to him, "Rise and go. Your faith has made you well." Jesus knew this man's heart and he knew he had healed 10, despite asking the questions.

The man overwhelmed with God's grace, just fell to his feet, and continued to thank the Son of God. Not only had this man been healed physically, but by his faith and thanksgiving to Jesus Christ, he was healed spiritually.

All 10 Lepers were obedient to the command Jesus gave them. All 10 were healed. The passage doesn't tell us if the Lepers questioned Jesus as to why they needed to go to the priests, they just did what Jesus told them to do. Jesus had a reputation for healing and compassion. Perhaps that is why the Lepers did not question anything. Healing begins with believing that Jesus can heal, then crying out to God just as the Lepers had done. Yet, it is through obedience where the healing occurs in this story. I find it difficult to be obedient to God in general. The flesh and self are in constant conflict with the Spirit.

The Leper who returned to Jesus, was a foreigner. Being a foreigner and expressing so much gratitude (loudly) surprised Jesus even more. Not only had the Leper been obedient to Jesus' command and experienced physical healing, but because he returned to the Lord and gave thanks, he was made whole. I think about this often. It was through praise and thanksgiving the man was made whole spiritually. I want to be like the Leper that returned to Jesus because of his faith.

As beautiful as this story is, for whatever reason, sometimes healing does not occur. Ultimately, God decides who is healed. I've struggled with the death of close friends who needed healing. I struggled with the death of my daughter, Eden Leigh Fry, who was born dead. Death is dark and can be overwhelming, but as believers it does not have the final say in our lives.

We have to believe he knows what is best. Does this mean we shouldn't pray for healing? Absolutely not, we should always pray for healing in others. We should also pray for healing in ourselves. If we are blessed to experience miraculous healing (physically or emotionally), we should give thanks to the Lord just as the Leper did. We must also remember this world is temporary and our physical bodies will eventually disintegrate into the earth, but spiritually we have a whole other life to live that goes beyond our comprehension.

Read Luke 17:11-19

Eldon E. Fry and Marc A. Fry

The Long Journey from Head to Heart

(by Eldon Fry)

EVEN AS A THREE-YEAR-OLD, I KNEW THE WOOD BURNING stove at my grandparents' home was to be avoided. However, I rode my tricycle through the kitchen and bumped into the stove and the hot lid landed on my fingers gripping the handles of my tricycle. I learned a very permanent lesson and still carry the scars that journeyed from a knowledge of warning to the reality of pain and scarring. Although not always dramatic, the journey from head to heart can be a long-distance pilgrimage.

There are many things I know could be painful but knowledge does not always guide my heart from the potential danger they hold. Even the simple ten commandments, which I had to memorize as a child, reside in my memory but they are not always honored in my heart. I write of a heart that is the center of emotions, giftedness, strengths, personality, and other basis for daily living. I carry the scars on my hand as a permanent reminder that knowledge is essential, but it needs to transfer to my heart.

Recently our Surgeon General in the United States declared that we are experiencing a national pandemic. Not from an unleashed virus but a pandemic of loneliness. Once we have broken the ties of living in communities of birth, moved out of office buildings, left our cubicles to work from home or coffee shops, and meet people only through social media or other tech platforms. I know that community is valuable and helpful in my personal growth and development but emotionally I find it easier to isolate than do the work of community building. As the Surgeon General noted, reluctance to interact with others can be the root cause of a pandemic of loneliness.

I have had several conversations with people who felt alone or are experiencing a significant degree of loneliness. God created us with a desire for relationships, God honored that need by relating with us as well as providing other people in our lives. We are not alone in this journey. God in great mercy has also provided other people that relate to our lives. I look back over the week and know that I have benefited from the interactions of others. The friend who helped me, the individual who gave their expertise to help me accomplish a goal, the person who took time for a real conversation, the one who walked by and laid his hand on my shoulder, the stranger who volunteered his time and then the person who invited me to share my gifts with others.

It was helpful to pause and remember that I am not alone at all. I thought I was alone and that created an aura of loneliness. I am only alone if I choose to separate myself from others. Alone never! Unless I choose to isolate myself. It is good to stop and reflect on how "un-alone" I really am. Right now, I recall a childhood hymn whose words proclaim, "How can I be lonely?" Great question! I don't think I am or at least I can travel from the idea of aloneness and separate myself from others, but the journey of the heart embraces those moments of interaction where I am not alone from an ever-present God or others in my life.

While it may have been a long journey from head to heart, it is a pleasant one to realize I am in community with others. I do not need a scar to remind me what I know about the necessity of relationships. I just need to identify and act on the opportunities.

The Light

(by Marc Fry)

THE LIGHT SHINES IN THE DARKNESS, BUT THE DARKNESS HAS *not overcome it. (John 1:5)*

There is a type of darkness where shadows still exist, and then there is darkness where you can't even see your hand in front of your face. All darkness is devoid of light to some degree. The darkest place I have ever experienced was deep inside a cave. Once you have gone deep into a cave and have turned off your light, it immediately gets dark and completely silent. It really is quite an experience.

Spiritually speaking, darkness is all around us. It is prevalent in this world. All of us will experience a level of darkness at some point during our lifetime. Many will experience more darkness than others. Some will actually choose to live in darkness, while others are desperate to get away from it. Darkness can be traumatic, full of fear, and depressing. Death, loss, sadness, oppression, disappointment, addiction, sickness, and anger are all associated with darkness. Hell is often described as a place of darkness, where there is no hope.

Living in this world is only temporary. Time will pass by very quickly. Life can be very difficult. Unless you have purpose or faith in God, it all will all pass away. Satan is very active and spiritual warfare is real. There is a constant battle between good and evil. Sometimes it plays out right before our eyes with terrorism and terrible acts that occur on the innocent. The good news is that even in the darkest of places the smallest ray of light can pierce the darkness. Once light, even the smallest degree, has pierced darkness, hope begins to reside.

Jesus is referred to as the Light. It is because of Jesus Christ that we can have hope, even in the darkest situations of life. I will not pretend to know why or understand why so many bad things can happen to people (other than Satan wanting to destroy as many lives as possible). Despite whatever difficult circumstances, people survive, thrive, and display incredible faith in God.

Corrie Ten Boom and her family sheltered Jews during the reign of Hitler. Eventually Dutch citizens informed the Germans. All of Corrie Ten Boom's family were arrested and sent to concentration (death) camps. Corrie and her sister Betsy were sent to Ravensbruck outside of East Berlin. Betsie was killed at the death camp but Corrie survived and was eventually rescued towards the end of the war. Despite the tragedy, loss, fear, sadness, and anger experienced, she never lost her faith or love for the Lord. Joni Erickson Tada was paralyzed shoulders down, at age 17, after diving into shallow water. Her active outdoor lifestyle ended that day. However, she has never given up on life or on God. She has had an impact on millions of people with her paintings, books, movies, and ministry to disabled persons from all over the world. She is now in her 60s, and was recently diagnosed with breast cancer. She recently stated that she was anxious to see how God is going to use her through this illness.

How do people survive such darkness? I can't imagine too many more low points in life than what was experienced by these two women of faith. Their testimony is incredible and inspiring. The light inside them is strong and there is little room for darkness, despite their circumstances. I want to think I could respond to such tragedies as they have, but my faith isn't there yet. The Bible does tell us (In Psalms) that we will walk through the valley of the shadow of darkness. It also tells us (in James) to stand strong because **after** we have suffered, he will restore us. My lifetime verse is Colossians 1:13-14, "For He has rescued me from the dominion of darkness, and placed me into the kingdom of his son, in whom we have redemption and forgiveness of sins." The light is always available. It is ready to pierce the darkness and provide sight and direction to the path. It is our choice as to whether we are going to look for the light, seek it and embrace it.

John 1:1 - 14

Visions and Dreams

(by Eldon Fry)

JOEL 2:25-32. NEW LIVING TRANSLATION

²⁵ The Lord says, "I will give you back what you lost to the swarming locusts, the hopping locusts, the stripping locusts, and the cutting locusts.[a]It was I who sent this great destroying army against you. Once again you will have all the food you want, and you will praise the Lord your God, who does these miracles for you. Never again will my people be disgraced. Then you will know that I am among my people Israel, that I am the Lord your God, and there is no other. Never again will my people be disgraced. [b]"Then, after doing all those things, I will pour out my Spirit upon all people. Your sons and daughters will prophesy. Your old men will dream dreams, and your young men will see visions. In those days I will pour out my Spirit even on servants—men and women alike. And I will cause wonders in the heavens and on the earth—blood and fire and columns of smoke. The sun will become dark, and the moon will turn blood red before that great and terrible[c] day of the Lord arrives. But everyone who calls on the name of the Lord will be saved, for some on Mount Zion in Jerusalem will escape, just as the Lord has said. These will be among the survivors whom the Lord has called.

Acts 2:17-21, 41 New Living Translation
'In the last days,' God says, 'I will pour out my Spirit upon all people. Your sons and daughters will prophesy. Your young men will see visions, and your old men will dream dreams. In those days I will pour out my Spirit even on my servants—men and women alike—and they will prophesy. And I will cause wonders in the heavens above and signs on the earth below—blood and fire and clouds of smoke. The sun will become dark, and the moon will turn blood red before that great and glorious day of the Lord arrives. But everyone who calls on the name of the Lord will be saved.'[a] 41 Those who believed what Peter said were baptized and added to the church that day—about 3,000 in all.

"Visions and Dreams: Embracing God's
Spirit for Transformation"

In the tapestry of life, we encounter the enigmatic realms of dreams and visions, each holding a distinct essence that shapes our journeys as church and business leaders. As we delve into the depths of these experiences, we unearth profound insights into our purpose and destiny. Dreams, with their whimsical and unconventional nature, invite us to transcend the boundaries of conventional thinking, challenging norms and embracing boundless creativity. Rooted in our past experiences and convictions, dreams serve as reflections of our innermost desires, guiding us towards fulfilling God's plan.

On the other hand, visions ignite a spark of optimism and a future-oriented perspective. They act as beacons of light, guiding us with unwavering clarity towards our goals. Some may view visions as the domain of the young, driven by stamina, energy, and hustle. However, we come to realize that dreams and visions know no age, for they reside in the hearts of all who dare to dream.

As we reflect on Peter's powerful sermon on the day of Pentecost, we find hope in the promise of the outpouring of God's Spirit upon all people. In this generation, regardless of age, gender, or social status, the Spirit brings the gift of prophecy to help us discern God's love and receive His message with insight for today's world. This revelation shatters stereotypes of prophets, as all who receive the Spirit become translators of God's love through their connection to Him.

Joel, an unexpected prophet, once prophesied about a devastating invasion of locusts, bringing loss, hunger, terror, and hopelessness. Yet, in the midst of despair, Joel declared God's promise: "I will give you back what you lost to the swarming locusts." A miraculous restoration in ordinary times, where sons and daughters, influenced by the Spirit, lead the way.

As we navigate through different seasons of life, we find significance in Joel's distinction: "Your old men will dream dreams, and your young men will see visions." In the twilight of life, dreams may guide our steps, offering insights and wisdom. Simultaneously, we celebrate the visions of the young leaders, who are motivated by the Spirit to act in new, innovative ways, accomplishing God's work in the context of today.

In this convergence of dreams and visions, the Spirit flows, flooding those on the margins, irrespective of gender, with divine inspiration and guidance. Let us embrace God's Spirit with open hearts, allowing dreams to inspire us and visions to propel us forward. As church and business leaders, we can be catalysts for transformation, bringing hope, joy, and the fulfillment of God's promises to our communities and beyond. With the outpouring of the Spirit upon us, we stand united, embarking on a transformative journey, aligning our aspirations with God's divine plan, and discovering the extraordinary path laid before us.

What a way to begin a ministry! Peter preached his first recorded sermon on the day of Pentecost. The results have not been duplicated! (Acts 2:41 *"Those who believed what Peter said were baptized and added to the church that day—about 3,000 in all."*) I pray that happens as a result of your ministry! It may not be 3000 at one time but over time there would be those amazing responses that changes lives.

We live in a time where the promise of outpouring of God's Spirit upon *"all people"* gives me hope for this generation. Regardless of age, gender or social status the Spirit will deluge all people bringing the much-needed gift of prophesy so that people can discern God's love and receive God's message with insights for today's world. This message seemed to destroy the stereotype I had of prophets. They are not all wild-eyed John the Baptist or the dramatic and marginalized Jeremiah or the even keeled and respected Isaiah. All receiving this new experience became translators of God's love "through our connection to him." (Shawn Bolz p. 18)

Joel was never a Jewish preferred prophet. He had prophesied about a pestilence of locusts who invaded the land in unprecedented numbers. Joy was lost, hunger invaded the land, terror and hopelessness gripped the land. Joel could declare :25 *"The Lord says, 'I will give you back what you lost to the swarming locusts....'"* Hope would return and expectations would be realized. A miracle in ordinary time! Sons and daughter would lead the way under the Spirit's influence.

I see that happening and it gives me great hope. Then Joel makes some distinctions that I find very real in my own life as he declares, *"Your old men will dream dreams, and your young men will see visions."* I realize that in this seventy-seventh year of my life, with my body more frail and less active that I see potential and dream dreams. However, I am more measured in my steps now and experience debilitating pain in action. I still value the wisdom of "dreams" and the insights they bring. However, I truly celebrate the "visions" of the young men and women who lead with great insight and are motivated by the Spirit to act in new ways to accomplish God's work in today's context. The Spirit literally is flooding those on the margins both male and female.

During times of leadership transitions or succession, the weight of responsibility and the question of legacy and identity often bubble to the surface. it is worth noting that around 70% of leadership successions, both in the corporate and non-profit sectors, fail to achieve the desired outcomes. In the midst of such challenges, spiritual practices can play a pivotal role in supporting leaders during this season of change. Two such practices are centering prayer (a form of contemplative prayer that involves letting go of thoughts and emotions to rest in the presence of God) and lectio divina (meaning "divine reading," is a method of prayerful reading and meditation on sacred scriptures) These practices can be extremely helpful for leaders as they navigate through transitions, providing solace, clarity, and strength in their pursuit of discerning God's will for the path ahead.

Bethesda

(by Marc Fry)

IN JERUSALEM, THERE WAS A SERIES OF POOLS CALLED BETHESDA.
The two pools were located near an entrance known as the
Sheep Gate. This pool area had 5 large porches or porticos
where large groups of people who were lame, paralyzed, blind or
considered to be invalids remained. It was believed that healings
had occurred at the pools, so people were waiting for the water
in the pool to move. When the waters were stirred, it was known
that the first person to enter was healed from their affliction
supernaturally. The healing pools derived from Greek culture
and was considered a paganistic ritual. Being an invalid (persons
with disabilities, injuries or disease) there was little hope for
healing, so the pools attracted many desperate people.

Bethesda means house of Mercy. It was here at Bethesda
that Jesus entered the paganistic area to meet the disabled face
to face. One man had been an invalid for 38 years. Jesus knew
his suffering, yet he asked the man, "Do you want to be healed?"
The man did not answer (yes or no) but rather he began to reveal
his inability to enter the pool when the waters were stirred. He
was incapable of seeking healing by himself because he did not
have the help he needed.

I can't help but think that the man had grown so accustomed to his lifestyle that he couldn't really relate to the time when he was healthy anymore. 38 years is a long time to wait and hope for healing. I think of people who have unchangeable physical disabilities, and people with addictions who have struggled throughout life and continue down the path they have been on for so long. Hope has been stifled. Healing is beyond comprehension. The path they have been on has become "who they are" and who they "identify" themselves as. I have found myself in this same situation, not as an "invalid" but as a person who has struggled with an addiction throughout my life. Many people go through life in need of healing not only physically but emotionally.

Jesus had compassion on the man despite his response. Jesus told him to get up, to take his bed and to walk. The man obeyed and departed the area only to be questioned by religious leaders who were concerned that it was Jesus who had healed him on the Sabbath.

Where do we go for healing? God has provided people who are of incredible skill and knowledge as doctors and scientists. To not use the resources God has provided to us would not be rational and careless. Yet do we seek God first through the situations we might find ourselves in, or loved ones might be experiencing? Do we ask for his guidance? There is power in Jesus Christ. He overcame death. He provides us with direction, knowledge, mercy, peace, provision and even healing when we seek him.

I know for me; it is only when I humble myself and seek the Lord's grace that I experience peace in my life regardless of any situation. Thirty-eight years of waiting for the water to stir and for someone to help you enter the water is a long time. I have often had to ask myself these questions; Do I really want to be healed? Do I want to be rescued from my discouraged emotional state? Do I want to be delivered from bondage? Whether or not we experience emotional or physical healing in this life, we can be delivered from death by coming to Jesus and asking him to take control of our lives as sinners in a fallen world.

Read John 5:1-17

Eldon E. Fry and Marc A. Fry

Attention

(by Eldon Fry)

HAVE YOU HAD THAT MOMENT WHERE YOU WERE SURPRISED by someone and "What happened to you!" just escaped from all the barriers on your mouth? I recall very good friends who drove through flooded streets one night. They turned onto a flooded street and splashed into deep water while going too fast. The street water shot up through the rusty floor boards and covered our friends with the leaves that had accumulated in their convertible that was now mixed with the muddy water from the street. Those words escaped the trap my brains had placed on my lips and I heard myself exclaiming, "What happened to you?" along with laughter. Fortunately, our friends were laughing, too. I recently read a bestselling book entitled, What Happened to You. Most of us experience these moments in our lives that are often pivot points with either positive and negative results. Some are very dramatic, others are more subtle and demand an awareness on our part to realize that we need to give our attention to them.

Some things in life simply require our attention. Exodus three recalls the story of Moses minding his father-in-law's sheep in a remote area of the desert near Mount Horeb when he saw a burning bush that was not being destroyed. "So Moses thought, 'I will go over and see this strange sight—why the bush does not burn up.'" (Exodus 3:3). That act of paying attention opened a personal invitation by God for Moses to step into a leadership role. It changed the course of his life and that of the enslaved Israelites in Egypt. In Luke 12 Jesus notes that attentiveness can help bring life into perspective. He says, "Consider the ravens…(verse 24) then reminds his audience to "Consider how the lilies grow.(verse 27) to help his followers to be more aware of their surroundings that give a perspective on their battle with worry. The scripture uses the word "consider" to draw attention to life changing perspectives on investment in land (Proverbs 31:16) and to urge us to acknowledge the great things God has done (I Samuel 12:24). The Psalmist 8:3 encourages us to consider the heavens and the work of creation to teach us humility because the Lord is majestic. Paul and Timothy reaffirm the value of humility in the letter to the Philippians 2:3 and 3:8 as a means to live in good relationship to one another.

Life is filled with experiences but to live those events and not consider or reflect on their meaning is to miss an important opportunity for growth especially in our inner life. These experiences serve as a basis for our formation and guides for our life choices. Sleepwalking through our life results in stunted growth. Watchfulness and awareness prioritizes each situation as an opportunity for Christian formation. It follows the pattern of Jesus who would notice an olive tree and provide a powerful lesson on fruitfulness and would heal someone and provide a lesson on gratefulness and thankfulness.

Life is the one space we have opportunity to notice, to be mindful and see with our eyes and hear with our ears and allow that to impact our souls. I have been stunned when I asked people who have great experiences what they learned from those experiences when I realize they had not learned anything significant enough to share with me.

Q. What has caught your attention lately? Did you pay attention or rush on by it?

The Stoning at Lystra

(by Marc Fry)

PAUL'S MINISTRY INCLUDED SPEAKING TO BOTH JEWS AND Greeks. He once was a Jew with great authority, and he intensely persecuted Christians. After his incredible conversion experience with Jesus, he aggressively pursued sharing the gospel without fear. Both Paul and Barnabas made their way into what is now known as Turkey. In Turkey, they encountered mostly Greeks but some Jews and Gentiles as well. As we all know, Greeks followed pagan Gods (Greek Mythology).

Both Paul and Barnabas displayed the power given to them through the Holy Spirit. They were able to heal people and lead them to salvation in Christ. After healing a man who was crippled in his feet, they referred to Paul as the Greek God, Hermes, and they referred to Barnabas as Zeus. The man they healed had been crippled and unable to walk since birth. An overwhelming majority of people in the crowd (including a sacrificial priest of Zeus) were stirred up and insisted on making sacrifices to Paul and Barnabus because of the miraculous act. Animals were quickly gathered, and the ritual sacrifice began to be put into motion even though Paul and Barnabas emphatically insisted not to follow through with the sacrifices and continued to claim that God has created all things. They preached that

God allowed his son to be sacrificed for anyone who wants to believe in him. The crowds became unmanageable and were barely able to be restrained.

It was at that time some of the Jews, who had been following Paul and Barnabas, began to stir up the crowds against them. These Jewish leaders were preaching that one must become a Jew and follow Jewish traditions before becoming a Christian. Somehow, they were able redirect the energy of the crowd into anger and rage towards Paul despite the miracle that had taken place. Eventually the crowds dragged Paul out of the city and stoned him until they thought he was dead. Once the stoning ceased, the crowds left. The disciples gathered around Paul. Paul eventually regained his strength and departed with Barnabus to go to another city known as Derbe to continue to share the gospel.

After preaching in Derbe, Paul went back to Lystra (*the place where he just was stoned almost to death*)! Why would he even consider going back to a city where they had just attempted to take his life in a horrific method? Paul had a calling on his life. He was determined to be obedient to the Lord even to death. He was burdened to return and encourage the disciples and to demonstrate how to have no fear. Paul displayed confidence in doing whatever the Lord had called him to do.

Paul eventually went on to be stoned multiple times because of his desire to take the path God had led him to. He was whipped, shipwrecked, thrown in prison, yet he continued his calling of being an apostle, and praised God despite the hardships. Jesus tells us in John 16:33, "I have told you these things so that you will have peace. In this world you will have troubles, but take heart, I have overcome the world." Following Jesus is not an easy thing to do. Being an apostle or disciple of Jesus requires much discipline. If we choose to seek God's calling on our life, there is nothing that can keep us from fulfilling his path for us, other than ourselves. Let us seek God with our whole heart and let us have no fear.

Read Acts 14:1-28

I Need a Shephard

(by Eldon Fry)

I NEED A SHEPHERD! A SHEPHERD IS ONE WHO LEADS A FLOCK by going before them. While in Israel, I watched a shepherd lead the way for sheep to the green pastures in a rock filled land. However, a hireling drove the sheep to the chosen location. I need a shepherd who leads the way by going before me, not someone driving me. That imagery fills the biblical text. Although we seldom see shepherds today, it was a common experience for people of Israel to understand.

Several years ago, Bill and Gloria Gaither wrote and sang a beautiful prayer/song entitled "Gentle Shepherd." The song begins,

> "Gentle Shepherd come and lead us for we need
> you to help us find our way Gentle Shepherd
> come and feed us for we need your strength from
> day to day
>
> There's no other we can turn to Who can help us
> face another day
>
> Gentle Shepherd come and lead us for we need to
> you to help us find our way."

It is New Year's Day, and this song is our prayer amidst the confusion, chaos and challenges that looking at the future creates. There are multiple question marks for the coming year but that is not unusual. The child Jesus was a refugee in Egypt from Israel a land dominated by a foreign country, Rome. The whim of a Roman ruler had increased taxes demanding travel to home towns, multiple children aged two and under were murdered to protect the throne of Herod. To this day there is an identification with the tears of Rachel weeping for the loss of children. The horror was unimaginable and confusion of where places of safety existed was not available for many and the scenario continued to be dangerous.

Shepherds were not considered proper in society. They could not attend temple services or witness in court. Yet one of Israel's heroes was King David, known as the Shepherd King. As if that was not signal enough that God was able to turn society upside down, the birth of Jesus according to Luke 2 was announced and attended by shepherds from the hill country outside Bethlehem. Truly God was disrupting the social order of Israel and giving the marginalized a voice and hope against all the fears of a people in bondage and domination of Rome emperors and their rule. Jesus made it plain in John 10 that those whose faith was in God, not the power of Rome, were favored to have a shepherd who knew their names (:14) and would lay down his life for them (:15). As a result of being known and cared for by a gentle shepherd, the sheep would listen to his voice (:27)

King David, the Shepherd King, would pen the words of Psalm 23 known widely and quoted even at funerals. "The Lord is my shepherd, I shall not be in want. He makes me to lie down in green pastures, he leads me beside quiet waters, he restores my soul. He guides me in paths of righteousness for his name's sake." Even fear would vanish because of trust in the shepherd. If you have opportunity, watch a herd of sheep led by a good shepherd. They walk with confidence and trust believing in the leadership of the shepherd. It seems like an appropriate prayer to pray for a shepherd of that sort to lead us today. Little wonder that the writer of Hebrews refers to Jesus (Hebrews 13:20) as "... that great Shepherd of the sheep..."

An older hymn (1779) plaintively invites Christ as "Savior like a shepherd lead us. Much we need thy tender care." Some people are offended that we are compared to sheep. Yet we like sheep lose our way without a shepherd, (I Peter 2:25) "For you were like sheep going astray, but now you have returned to the Shepherd and Overseer of your souls."

Q. What are indications of your return to the Shepherd? How is the Shepherd leading you?

Flee

(by Marc Fry)

As a Christian we have freedom in the way we pray, we worship, what we eat, who we associate with, what we choose to do, and the list goes on and on. This is one of the main reasons I choose to be a Christian, because of the freedom we have as a believer. Our freedom goes beyond the law, it includes freedom over death. Because of Jesus, we have freedom over death and direct access to God through prayer.

The Bible discusses the choices we have. Paul states this very clearly, "All things are lawful for me, but not all things are helpful. All things are lawful for me, but I will not be dominated by anything." These verses are very powerful. Prior to the sacrifice of Jesus, laws were restraining on people. Religious leaders took the law to a whole other level. When Jesus died on the cross, the binding of the law lost its power over believers. As mentioned before, after the resurrection of Jesus, we now can have a direct relationship with God. The law is not irrelevant, but it does not have control over our relationship with God.

The freedom we have allows us options and choices, but not everything is good for us. Some things can take us away from communication with the Lord and begin to dominate our lives. Money, Sex, Alcohol, Work, Shopping, Sports, Emotions,

Relationships, and Family can consume our time and some of these can turn into addictions that lead us down very destructive paths.

Paul takes time to discuss sexual immorality and specifically tells us to flee from it. Sexual immorality is having sexual relations with others outside of marriage. He continues to tell us how destructive sexually immoral relationships can be. Our body belongs to the Lord, he created us and if we are a believer, his spirit lives within us. When we go outside of marriage for sexual desires and sexual cravings it can be very destructive and can quickly control our lives, finances and thought patterns. I have been down this path and it has been very destructive in my life. The blessings God has given me in the past were often stolen by acting on the desires and cravings I had. In my book "The Struggle" (available on Amazon), I get into more detail of how destructive patterns became a part of my life.

There is a battle for our soul. Our soul is where our mind, emotions and spirit reside. When we open ourselves up to destructive things, our mind and body can experience bondage. Paul encourages us to be joined with the Lord (I Corinthians 6:17) rather than things that will complicate our life or pull us away from our relationship with him.

If you read through, 1st and 2nd Samuel, 1st and 2nd Kings, and 1st and 2nd Chronicles (in the Old Testament), there were more bad kings than there were good kings for both Israel and Judah. The good kings removed the idols of worship, and some went into the high places, destroyed the Asherah Poles, and crushed the stones of worship to help the people turn away from their sin and confusion.

Jesus says, "I have come so that you might have life and have it abundantly (John 10:10)." We have the option to turn from temptation and even to flee situations when they have been presented to ourselves. We have the option to be obedient, disciplined in our thoughts and actions, and choose to pursue a close relationship Jesus. When we do this, we can experience freedom within the parameters he has given us.

Read 1 Corinthians 6:12-18

Nurturing a Soul

(by Eldon Fry)

"The great illusion of leadership is to think that man can be led out of the desert by someone who has never been there."

Henri Nouwen, *The Wounded Healer*

"HE (LORD) RESTORES MY SOUL." PSALM 23:3

It was a Junior High growth spurt. My family moved for one year to Twin Falls, Idaho to help a struggling church plant. When I returned to northern Idaho a year later and began classes at Kendrick, Idaho, I had grown from a chubby 5'7"to a gangly 6'2". I could no longer wear my old jeans. I no longer responded to "Shorty" or "Fatso." Even my feet had grown to size 12 from size 8! I began to discover a new world athletically, and while swimming in puberty awkwardly felt new urges in awareness of sexuality and discovered the necessity and reality of work for pay. Now I could drive on the farm, work a small acreage from planting to harvest and even enter the world of scholastic politics. Although I was a "mountain boy" there was new respect by upper class men and women. I needed some role models to help me navigate the confusing messages of High School. Faith and church seemed like an unrelated necessity in my understanding and an act of obligation for my family. With no one leading the way, except the example of my grandfather, my soul withered by irrelevancy while my opportunities and body flourished. Growth spurts can result in initial awkwardness and surprising results.

How can I nurture my soul? David Benner (*Care of Souls p22)"...we do not have a soul, we are soul." A page later he talks about "health of the inner person."* The scriptures speak of restoring my soul (Psalm 23) and that humans become *"living souls"* (Genesis 2:7). But our souls come with a warning, *"What good is it for a man to gain the whole world, yet forfeit his soul?"* (Mark 8:38 NIV) How do I feed my soul so that I am whole and healthy in my spiritual development? I had no answers in the wilderness of my teen years. The lack of answers brought me to rejection of religion in any form. It just seemed irrelevant and confusing. Early church leaders "fathers and mothers" led by word and example. It seems there are four elements in nurturing the soul. Sustaining practices (like an athlete) helps a person "endure and transcend a circumstance and prepare for spurts of growth to new opportunities. It should include reconciling, the restoration of broken relationships as well as receiving guidance from those who have gathered wisdom along the way. In summary Benner (page 32, 33,34) identifies six conclusions:

1. *Christian soul care is something we do for each other, not to ourselves.*
2. *Christian soul care operates within a moral context.*
3. *Christian soul care is concerned about community not just individuals.*
4. *Christian soul care is provided through dialogue within a relationship.*

5. *Christian soul care addresses the whole person. (Physical, spiritual, mental, psychological)*
6. *Christian soul care cannot be relegated to clergy.*

Where did I discover care for the soul? I discovered God was seeking me. There were some very simple practices that began to develop my spiritual muscles and heart strength. I discovered what might come natural and fill my developing longings. I learned to not chase my feelings or even my heart but began to pay attention to my soul.

Nurturing my soul began with spiritual transformation I could call my own and strengthened that change by building practices into my life out of love for the one I am following now, Jesus Christ. Much of what is packaged in self-help and psychotherapy today is repackaged Judeo-Christian belief in confession, repentance, prayer, faith, inner resolution, and groupings of like- minded people. It sets the table for a spiritual growth spurt.

Earlier I mentioned my grandfather. He modeled in word and deed intentionally to connect and care for his soul and as a result overflowed into mine. He was an unappointed mentor as I watched and worked with him on a daily basis. He said very little but spoke volumes by his values and decisions. Little did I realize that I was being nurtured in my soul. Later, I developed practices like I saw him model. I was drawn to read a Psalm several times then place myself in the Psalm and pray it as my own. I learned to journal around key words that stood out to my soul from the rest of the text. I began to grow as my neglected soul began to find new life and discover a very present God with us.

Source:

Benner, David G. *Care of Souls: Revisioning Christian Nurture and Counsel.*
Baker Books, Grand Rapids, MI. 1998.
Gaultiere, Bill and Kristi. *Journey of the Soul.*
Revell. Grand Rapids, MI. 2021

Fruit of the Spirit

(by Marc Fry)

"BUT THE FRUIT OF THE SPIRIT IS LOVE, JOY, PEACE, PATIENCE, *kindness, goodness, faithfulness, gentleness, self-control; against such things there is no law. And those who belong to Christ Jesus have crucified the flesh with its passions and desires. If we live by the Spirit, let us also keep in step with the Spirit."*

(Galatians 5:22-25 NIV)

Love

- let love be genuine (Romans 12:9)
- love is patient and kind (1 Corinthians 13:4)
- love your neighbor (James 2:8)
- perfect love casts out fear (1 John 4:18)
- love covers a multitude of sins (1 Peter 4:8).

Joy

- the joy of the lord is your strength (Nehemiah 8:10)
- joy comes in the morning (Psalms 30:5)
- He fills us with joy and peace (Romans 15:13)
- No one will take your joy from you (John 16:22)
- Make a joyful noise to the Lord (Psalms 100:1)

Peace

- He will keep in perfect peace whose mind is stayed on you (Isaiah 26:3)
- Strive for peace with everyone (Hebrews 12:14)
- Our God is not a God of confusion but of peace (1 Corinthians 14:33)
- The effect of righteousness is peace (Isaiah 32:17)
- Blessed are the peacemakers (Matthew 15:9)

Patience

- Be patient in tribulation (Romans 12:12)
- Be patient with the weak (1Thessalonians 5:14)
- Display his perfect patience towards others (1 Timothy 1:16)
- We have been called to be patience (Ephesians 4:2)
- The Lord is patient with us (2 Peter 3:9)

Kindness

- Be kind to one another (Ephesians 4:32)
- Kindness leads to life (Proverbs 21:21)
- The Lord is kind in all his works (Psalm 145:13)
- God has shown kindness to you (Romans 11:22)
- God will show us immeasurable grace through kindness (Ephesians 2:7)

Goodness

- Goodness and mercy will follow us (Psalms 23:6)
- How great is God's goodness (Zechariah 9:17)
- Let no one seek his own good, but the good of others (1 Corinth 10:24)

- All things work together for good (Romans 8:28)
- He who began a good work in you will complete it (Philippians 1:6)

Faithfulness

- His faithfulness is a shield (Psalm 91:4)
- Jesus said, "Have faith in God" (Mark 11:22)
- We walk by faith (2 Corinthians 5:7)
- Let us ask with faith (James 1:6)
- Be faithful unto death (Revelation 2:10)

Gentleness

- Learn from me, for I am gentle (Matthew 11:29)
- Have a gentle, quiet spirit (1 Peter 3:4)
- Restore others with gentleness (Galatians 6:1)
- Walk with humility and gentleness (Ephesians 4:2)
- Correct with gentleness (2 Timothy 2:25)

Self-control

- Be self-controlled, sober minded (1 Peter 4:7)
- Be a lover of good, self-controlled, upright (1 Timothy 1:8)
- We have not a spirit of fear, but of power, self-control (2 Timothy 1:7)
- Without self-control it is like a city broken into and left without walls (Proverbs 25:28)
- Have knowledge and self-control (2 Peter 1:6)

"But I say, walk by the Spirit, and you will not gratify the desires of the flesh."

(Galatians 5:16 NIV)

Hope on the Journey

(by Eldon Fry)

COUNSELORS AND PSYCHOLOGISTS, CHRISTIAN AUTHORS, spiritual leaders including Maya Angelou have noted that love succeeds in breaking through all barriers and allows us to attain our destination filled with hope to sustain us.

Hope seems more like an act of desperation than an assurance of confidence when you are born in the remote mountains of Idaho. It feels like the remark of Nathaniel, "Can anything good come out of Nazareth" (Southwick). Options are limited, education is often inferior and underappreciated, days are filled with the mundane chores of livelihood, extracurricular opportunities are seldom engaged, people suffer from "east coast bias," it is sparsely populated and often under resourced and it was identified as the least Christian portion of the United States. I find myself explaining that the characters I grew up with seemed a lot like those in Duck Dynasty except most families did not end their day with prayer. My surrounding culture and context was viewed as crude and without the cultural social graces of other parts of our country.

What hope does a child from that region have of being a difference maker or high achiever even in the "land of opportunity" our country purports? Hope is essential. To move through the barrier of survival focus into a thriving understanding of life that is not a false based optimism.

We can begin to rediscover hope. In the wildness and wilderness of Idaho, I found hope in the surrounding nature, the beauty of silence in the mountains, the resilience of forest burned or the rhythms of animal migrations. It was there that I could pause to listen to the "sounds of silence" around me and know that the songbirds spoke of hope, the beauty of a fawn and does, the majesty of elk, the reflection of fishing in a crystal-clear creek or river all spoke of hope and resilience of life even in the struggles for survival. Burned forests would burst with new life, the fish, bear and elk would replenish.

There is an inner sense of returning to belief in God because we are children drawn to return home where we are loved and celebrated. That is the fruit of the seeds of hope. Resilience is birthed in a hope that all is not lost even in tragedy. We can and will rebuild. I came to realize that even in my sin, I have the hope of repenting and changing the direction of my life. There is room for possibilities even in the challenging seasons that tempt us to despair in the swirling troubles that occur.

Society, especially western society, tends to be dominated by labels of "success" or "failure." People of hope live beyond and through those categories that dominate our western thinking and do the work of relabeling those identities that distinguish one group from another. We must not measure our success based on the evaluations and controls of petty fiefdom agendas. How can we be delivered from the tidal wave of society and the tsunami of being known as a success or failure?

Joshua's Path

(by Marc Fry)

JOSHUA WAS AN ISRAELITE BORN INTO SLAVERY IN EGYPT. HE was there when the people cried out to God for deliverance. He witnessed the 10 plagues. He saw Moses representing the people against Pharoah and being used by God. He was with the Israelites when they fled from Pharoah and his soldiers. Joshua saw how God used Moses in parting the Red Sea. His feet walked across the dry bed of the sea with walls of water on the sides. He saw the miracles performed and followed the leadership of Moses. Joshua was called upon to lead the fight against the Amalekites. Joshua was called upon to go up Mount Sanai with Moses. We all know how Joshua was selected as one of the 12 spies (one from each tribe of Israel) to go into the Promised land and return with a report.

It was only Joshua and Caleb who returned with an optimistic report. Ten of the spies feared the numbers of opposition, the size of those who were there and the fortified cities. Many of the people listened to the report of fear and began to complain to Moses and requested to go back to Egypt. Joshua and Caleb were stunned because they saw a land that was full of milk and honey. A land that had been prepared for them. The people were ready to stone them both because they refuted the testimony of the other 10. Surprisingly Moses begged the Lord not to wipe the people out. Those who were rebellious ended up dying in the wilderness and never saw the Promise Land.

Prior to the death of Moses, God had plans to use Joshua to lead the Israelites into the Promise Land. Moses was able to see it with his own eyes, but it was Joshua who led them into the land. It was Joshua who led the defeat Jericho with God's blessing and he saw the walls fall flat with his own eyes. Once in the Promised Land it was Joshua who gathered the Israelites to recount the goodness of God. He motivated them to seek the Lord, to confess their sins and to get rid of all idolatry. He said, "Choose this Day whom you will serve…as for me and my house, we will serve the Lord (Joshua 24)."

Joshua's testimony is amazing. The things he experienced and saw with his own eyes is like none other. He displayed so much confidence in God. He went from being born into slavery to leading the Israelites into the Promised Land. He was focused and ready to serve in whatever capacity. He had hope. He had a desire that was honorable. He didn't waiver in the things God led him to do. God prepared him for his role.

Sometimes I struggle to stay focused on the path. There are so many distractions, temptations and emotions along the way. Satan is ready to steal away your reward. He is ready to take away your joy and confidence. Frustration, disappointment, and doubt are always around the corner. The path to victory is not an easy path however, the path we take is ours to choose. We can fail and get lost very easily if we aren't prepared. The good thing is God's grace knows no boundaries. No matter how far we drift or get lost, there is always a way back to our relationship with God. The way back is through Jesus Christ. Choose this day.

Read Joshua 24:1-28

Remember the
Standing Stones

(by Eldon Fry)

MEMORIES FLOOD LIKE A TSUNAMI INTO OUR SOULS. THEY ARE not invited they just arrive at an overwhelming reality. We seem to literally return to that significant place locked in the closets of our minds that now seems present or like a long walk through the past. By traveling to the Middle East several times, I came to realize the importance in those cultures to remember. I was mesmerized by the rocks placed on the above ground stone burial caskets in cemeteries near Jerusalem. I realized that the flowers I placed on the gravesites of Idaho soon wilted and required replacement but rocks in a land filled with stones of all sizes seemed to be odd to my western mind. Then, it was explained to me that rocks symbolized that the person buried there would not be forgotten. Monasteries often contained an ossuary of the former priest's bones. It reminded all who passed by that there is a close connection between the living and the dead. Memory took on an added emotional symbolism to those who remain and remember. Often major events such as the crusades or other invasions are spoken of in words that indicate this could have happened yesterday or last week.

Memories play an important role in the soul path of those on the journey. In Deuteronomy 4:9,10 Moses reminds "...watch yourself closely so that you do not forget the things your eyes have seen or let them slip from your heart as long as you live."(:9) so they could teach these stories to their children and grandchildren and generations yet to be birthed. The next verse calls them to "remember"(:10) The lesson seems to be learned as Joshua leads the people across the Jordan, leaders from each tribe were to bring a stone from the middle of Jordan (Joshua 4) and built an altar of stones on the other side as a reminder to their children and grandchildren of God at work in their journey. One current ministry calls itself "Standing Stones Ministry" that is a call to remember and live into the miracles of God. Joshua 4:9 simply affirms "And they are there to this day." Which speaks of their importance and encouragement to the next generations.

While we cannot simply live in the memories of the past, they can reaffirm our current journey and teach us lessons of faith as we encounter the future. Each morning I spend several moments remembering a past experience of joy. It begins my day with a reframed view of life even in troubling times or a day of engaging chaos or other big issues. The lad, David could face his giant of the day, Goliath, because David had memories of God helping him face the lion and bear as he guarded his father's herd of sheep.

Jesus engaged in the culture of the Middle East and left this clear message to his followers called disciples. I Corinthians 11:24,25 "...do this in remembrance of me." Our broken memories need a reminder to remember. My great aunt shared that when a favorite song came on the radio (before Spotify) she would burst into tears as she remembered sharing the love of that song with her husband who had died earlier that year.

Reminders stir the memories from the shadows of our minds. It is critical in our spiritual path that we establish reminders to call us to remember those events that led us to this path and who it is that we are following. The one commandment that carries this marker is found in Exodus 20:8 "Remember the Sabbath day by keeping it holy." That memory would prevent the seventh day from becoming "just another day" in which to survive.

People, friends and community, can become those reminders to give thanks and to relate. Paul said it this way, "I thank my God every time I remember you." Our friendships can the "standing stones" to remind us of how God has blessed us with relationships and the value of shared experiences. That is crucial for those who journey on the path as long and challenging days merge into the ordinary of the daily. Jesus challenged his followers to allow the Spirit to "…remind you of everything I have said to you." (John 14:26)

Our celebrations that remind us of the words of Jesus and challenge each other to remain faithfully on the path are key to arriving at the goal of our faith.

Q. How do I serve as a reminder to follow Christ in the power of the Spirit?

The Cost

(by Marc Fry)

I REMEMBER AS A KID GOING TO A DAVID MEECE CONCERT IN Manhattan, KS. There was a song called "Count the Cost" that challenged the listener to make sure they really want to be a believer. The gift of having a relationship with God and salvation (Eternal Life) is free to anyone who chooses to do so. The price has already been paid by Jesus. He was whipped and beaten almost to the point of death. As if that wasn't enough, he was crucified on a cross and left to suffocate hanging up on a hill for everyone to see and to be mocked. However, death could not defeat him.

Luke 14 discusses the cost of discipleship. In verse 25 Jesus tells us, "If anyone comes to Me and does not hate his father and mother and wife and children and brothers and sisters, yes, and even his own life, he cannot be my disciple." Jesus did not hate his family, nor does Jesus want us to hate our families. Jesus did however leave his family to serve others and fulfill the purpose God had for him. Family was not #1, occupation was not #1, his own life was not #1, nor were the disciples #1, Jesus was focused on the will of God alone.

His focus was on helping the rejected, the handicapped, the widow, and the lost. His focus was so in tune with the will of God, that it cost him his life. Philippians 2:7-8 describes his approach in detail. It says, "But He emptied Himself, taking upon Himself the form of a servant, and was made in the likeness of men. And being found in the form of a man, He humbled Himself and became obedient to death, even death on a cross."

That is intense. Hopefully we will never have to experience persecution and death as followers of Jesus, but we may. Many people in the world already do. The disciples experienced terrible deaths. Peter was crucified upside down. James was stoned and clubbed to death. The list goes on except for John who managed to escape being a martyr (Christianity.com).

In Mark chapter 10 we find the rich man approaching Jesus and asking him what he must do to have eternal life. After discussing the commandments with him he tells the man to go and sell everything he has and give to the poor, and to take up his cross and follow him. The man turned and left grieving for he was a wealthy man.

Jesus was trying to prove a point that to be a true follower there is a cost. It might mean you don't have a house, it might mean you don't have a car, it might mean you live in a "not so good" neighborhood, it might mean you do not have a savings or a retirement account, it might mean you do not see your family very often, it might mean you live in a different culture, it might mean you are among people who have different values or religion than you. God loves all people and desires to reach those who need his love. We are his hands and feet. We need to have our eyes and ears open to his calling. Will we reach those who cross our paths? Will we be willing to sacrifice our own will for his? Will we be willing to look at things from an eternal perspective versus the here and now?

If you are a Child of God, he promises to take care of you, to provide for you, to meet your needs. It may not always be how we perceive it or want it to be, but he will provide for you, walk you through the fire and out the other side. The cost could be great, but the reward is beyond our own understanding.

The Voice of Nature

(by Eldon Fry)

NATURE IS A POWERFUL TOOL OF THE CHRISTIAN SPIRITUAL path. Often the poetry and metaphors of scripture utilize observations from nature. Romans 1:20 "For since the creation of the world God's invisible qualities—his eternal power and divine nature—have been clearly seen, being understood from what has been made, so that humans are without excuse." This text leaves little doubt that creation speaks powerfully to us of God and points out that we should worship the creator. In my visit to Israel and the desert lands especially those that are far from the lights of Jerusalem and Tel Aviv so that we can see clearly the radiant beams of the stars shining more brightly than elsewhere. Psalm 19:1-3 "The heavens declare the glory of God. The skies proclaim the work of his hands. Day after day they pour forth speech; night after night they display knowledge. There is no speech or language where their voice is not heard." Little wonder that the sights and sounds of the skies spoke to the king about the God he worshipped. Later, the Psalmist affirms, (Psalm 97:6) "The heavens proclaim his righteousness, and all the peoples see his glory."

I grew up in the "Big Sky Country of the west." Truly looking skyward seemed to speak of God and bring a closeness to the creator of the universe. My brother and I would sleep outside under those skies each summer and watch the dancing movement of northern lights and comets streaking across the darkened skies and the changing seasons marked by the different phases of the moon. Natures' voice left a definite impression on my soul even when the theology I heard from the pulpit did not relate to my life, nature clearly spoke of the existence of God. I recall hunting for deer and elk alone in the mountains of Idaho and coming to a vista that overlooked five mountain ranges. I was aware of a presence that did not fit my belief system but powerfully spoke to me of the existence of God. Let me be clear, nature is not God but nature is and can be a messenger of God. I recall riding my motorcycle up a mountain trail and pausing as I drove into an area with tree cover and filled with a herd of elk. I shut off my motorcycle and sat in reverent silence in what I recall as a cathedral of the holy.

Where do I go to avoid the voice of nature? Buildings built by humans can be glorious but do not speak with the same voice of a God present with us. Jesus challenged his followers to consider the lilies of the field that bloomed with unsurpassed beauty yet without the effort of "trying harder." The scripture is clear that we are not to live a lazy lifestyle but one that rests in trust of the one who is in control. God brings a sense of beauty to us through the ordinary visuals of nature.

While nature is beautiful and speaks of God, it also can be fierce and even destructive. We must be on alert and good stewards of that beauty. My grandfather, who never entered a church or cathedral, described his place of worship in nature. There are many treasured lessons to be learned from the mountains, the skies, the trees, the animals, even the hidden flowers and grass. Open them like a wonderful textbook as you travel the journey, and you will discover value that will speak to your soul as you reflect on their message.

Q. When have you experienced in God in nature?

Freedom

(by Marc Fry)

"FOR YOU SHALL KNOW THE TRUTH, AND THE TRUTH SHALL SET you free." John 8:32

What is truth? Even Caesar himself did not know as he stood face to face with Jesus. Unfortunately, we live in a world full of manipulation, half-truths, deception and lies. It can be very difficult to weed through fiction and find truth. It can even be very difficult to face the truth in our own lives. However, when we do discover the truth, it is like being around innocence. It helps bring about peace of mind and trust can be re-established.

Without truth there is no foundation, there is no freedom. One of the truths in the Bible that is imperative to grasp as a believer is that we have been set free from sin. How is this possible? If this is true, why do we still struggle? Why do our lives get filled with distractions and sin?

Jesus came to set us free from the law of sin and death (Romans 8:2). Without a Savior, we are all destined to experience the wages of sin, which eventually is death. All of us have sinned and will continue to deal with sin, that is reality. There are consequences of sin not just spiritually but by physical law. We should be thankful there are consequences, and we absolutely should have consequences for our actions. The difference is, as a believer there is no condemnation. God gives us grace. Jesus has paid the price and overcame death. Our identity is not tied to any sin or struggle we have or may experience. Our identity is in Christ.

We can have victory over sin in our lives when we surrender to God and seek to live by the Spirit, but if you are like me, it is a constant battle. Even Paul, possibly the most influential person in the scriptures, had a thorn in his flesh that he continually wrestled with.

Freedom in Christ involves surrendering our lives to Him, being obedient and pursuing holiness. This is counterculture to the "perceived freedom" of our society today in America. Sometimes I feel embarrassed for our society because of how we abuse the freedoms we have to the point where we think it is a right to do whatever we want in pursuit of pleasing ourselves. Hundreds of thousands of people sacrificed their lives in order for us to have the freedoms we have in America. It is disappointing to see Freedom not being respected or appreciated.

Scripture tells us not to use our freedom to indulge in the sinful nature and not for ourselves but rather to serve others in love (Galatians 5:13-14). How different would this world be if we respected freedom? If we understood what it means to have freedom in Christ? If we humbled ourselves and acknowledged God with thanksgiving for the freedoms we have?

Read Galatians 5:13-26

Wounded and Vulnerable

(by Eldon Fry)

AUTHENTIC FRIENDSHIP ON THE PATHWAY IS FOUND IN THE openness to each other. But for many reasons we allow our desire for safety to override our need to be vulnerable enough to form a community as we engage this journey. The result has been an epidemic of loneliness. We are on a path together but have not broken the barriers that exist that separate us. In 1972 a book by Henri J.M. Nouwen entitled *The Wounded Healer* became a "must read" book for Christians. Anywhere followers of Jesus gathered, this book soon became a part of the conversation. The idea that ministry could occur by revealing our wounds and addressing them would encourage healing in the lives of fellow travelers caught fire. Henri addressed ministers challenging them to reveal their own woundedness so that a fragmented culture could find a common bond that would provide healing. Like many cycles of popularity, the excitement of the moment faded and finally only served as a seldom revisited memory. Rather than allowing for the strengthening of our journey, the idea of a wounded healer served to help us realize the potential for pain when we become vulnerable or reveal our woundedness. Safety and security won the tension created and a majority of the followers of Jesus chose to shield themselves from sharing wounds or revealing vulnerability.

As a result of the backlash to vulnerability, loneliness and isolation has become so common that some health professionals call it "The Age of Loneliness" and assert it an epidemic. In an age of competition and rivalry competing for the top of the social ladder in business, social media, financial security and a deep desire to go viral with "Likes" and worship the heroes of our particular groupings, we begin to scatter *like sheep with no shepherd." (Matthew 9:36)*

Our garage doors become like ancient moats around our castles so no enemy can surprise us. Security has become big business. Items to keep us safe from interacting with others, especially unwanted others, sell well. "Be safe" is a common blessing to end conversations. Yet there does exist life intersections that allow us to interact in surprising opportunities. I recall meeting another family in Yellowstone Park and finding we had much in common and as Christians we had opportunity to share our stories, enjoy each other and leave the next day enriched by new friendships. For others it may be as simple as gathering mail at a condominium. While there are risks in hospitality, the potential benefit is breaking the isolation and loneliness. It does not always mean healing and freedom but hospitality provides potential for companionship on the journey. It combats the inner message that you are unique in your battles and no one else is experiencing similar challenges. James understood the concept in the early church, *"Confess your sins to each other so that you may be healed."(5:16)* Healing often arrives when I understand that I no longer need to hide my wounds behind a wall of shame but can share them along the journey and walk freely knowing I am not alone. The writer of Proverbs valued the *"wounds of a friend can be trusted."*

(Proverbs 27:6). There is an honesty and trustworthiness when a friend shares wounds that helps me identify my woundedness. When someone ignores the realities and wounds and only multiplies a false praise, we should look for the honesty of friendship for those who travel with us and be willing to reveal truth.

Q. When has hospitality to someone else created new awareness and hope in you?

Believe

(by Marc Fry)

THE FIG TREE THAT HAD NO FRUIT DISAPPOINTED JESUS. HE said, "Let this tree never bear fruit again." The fig tree withered away instantly. He then looked at the disciples and said if they have faith and no doubt, they could not only do what was done to the fig tree, but they could move mountains. Wow! Can you imagine the face of the disciples seeing the tree wither to nothing then Jesus saying they can do the same? What a powerful statement. I'm not sure I have ever had that kind of faith. I believe in Jesus, and I trust God but that is a whole different level he is talking about. Somehow doubt and disappointment tend to battle belief in my mind.

In Mark chapter 5 we find a woman who had been bleeding for 12 years. It says she had suffered under the care of many physicians. She had spent all the money she had seeking relief, but the condition only got worse. She heard of Jesus and believed in his ability to heal. She decided to pursue him and pushed her way through the crowds. As she got closer, she said to herself, "If only I could touch his garment, I might be healed." Eventually she was able to get close enough to the robe of Jesus, and she immediately felt a healing power travel throughout her body. Jesus, feeling power had left his body, asked, "Who touched me?" The woman was scared, but she fell to the feet of Jesus and told the truth. Jesus blessed her faith and honesty.

I do not understand how healing works, nor do I understand how some people are healed and others are not. I do know that God has a plan and a purpose for all people. I do know people have been healed miraculously and others have passed despite the prayers of many. This can be a very difficult thing to handle. Believing goes beyond healing, it goes into all areas of our lives.

In Matthew 19 Jesus was having a discussion with his disciples about being saved. He proceeded to tell them how difficult it is for a man of wealth to enter the Kingdom of Heaven. The disciples asked if a rich man cannot be saved, then who can? Jesus responded by telling them that, "...with God, all things are possible." If we believe that Jesus is the Son of God and overcame death, we can be saved and receive eternal life. God is capable of doing anything.

Despite whatever the circumstances might be, whatever the outcome is, and if our expectations are not met, will we still believe? Where do we put our trust? Is it in wealth? Is it in careers? Is it in the government? Is it in medicine and science? What if we could talk to Abraham, Moses, Joseph, David, Peter, James, John, Paul? What would they say? Would they encourage us to believe?

God performs miracles daily. It may not be as we want to perceive it, but they happen every day. The sun rises, and the sun sets. The leaves change colors and fall to the ground only to reappear on the branches again the next season. A seed is planted, the rain falls, and eventually something with life springs forth from the ground. Our bodies, when injured, will eventually heal. We have a soul and we are able to express and experience emotions, we are able to forgive and share love. God gives and takes away. He can provide what is needed in an instant. He is able to do more than we can even imagine. However, sometimes things don't go as planned, or we are disappointed with the outcomes. We can become angry, disappointed, and even turn away from God or even curse him.

The Bible tells us in proverbs to trust in the Lord with all our heart and to lean not on our own understanding. We don't always know how God works. Our beliefs are challenged. By humbling ourselves, and by acknowledging God, He is able to work in us through pain, difficulties, and loss. If we don't believe, or choose not to believe, we will pass by like the wind, invisible to others. Our lives will have very little purpose or hope. The bible tells us that a person who claims to believe but is filled with doubt is a like a double minded man that gets tossed about like a wave in the sea.

As I have matured it seems like there is more and more to fear, but there is also a peace we can have as a believer. With age comes the opportunity to have a deeper faith and to see what you really believe. An overwhelming majority of us have gone through something that has challenged our belief in God. It's usually not until later in life we can look back and see his faithfulness and potentially have a better perspective on the events that have shaped our faith.

Since God continually allows us to choose what we believe, I choose to believe in one man, the Son of God, who overcame death so that we might have life. What do you believe?

Read Hebrews Chapter 11

Care versus Cure

(by Eldon Fry)

IF WE ARE TRAVELING A DUSTY PATHWAY ATTEMPTING LIKE A child following a parent and walking in their footsteps which are a longer adult stride than childlike short legs can manage. It is easy to begin to imagine the lie that we, just like our Savior are responsible to cure everyone we encounter. Jesus put that myth to rest by one of his most famous stories known as the good Samaritan. A hated and marginalized outsider stops to care for a hated Jewish traveler. The traveler is Jewish and is badly beaten and robbed of his finances used for trade inn Jericho. It is a treacherous area and well known as an area to avoid if you travel alone. Religious people within his legitimate friendship and religious circle avoid the battered traveler and move on to their business in Jericho. But the Samaritan stops to care for the naked and beaten man with his own resources. The Samaritan sees what others have avoided but *"sees him and took pity on him." (Luke 10:33)* and *"...bandaged his wounds, pouring on oil and wine. Then he put the man on his own donkey, took him to an inn and took care of him." (:34).* The Samaritan paid the innkeeper to care for the following the wounded Jew and promised to reimburse any overage of expense in caring for the wounded man. Jesus was asked a significant question of a legal expert in the law, "Who is my neighbor?" The answer was too obvious to deny after Jesus shred this insightful story. It was obvious, that the neighbor was the one who had mercy on Jewish victim even though the helper was a hated Samaritan. Jesus simply stated that we should go and do likewise.

The wise man who wrote Proverbs declares, *"The righteous care about justice for the poor, but the wicked have no such concern." (Proverbs 29:7)* The message is clear for the travelers of the path. We are to care. We cannot always cure, we may not even see the cure take place and we may need to involve others in caring about our neighbors for there is need of those who cure but often it is initiated by those who care. Our opportunities to care may not be a singular person but someone caught in the whims of systems run amuck. We are following the footsteps of someone who modeled caring not just physical issues but the Psalmist notes that God *"heals the brokenhearted and binds up their wounds." (Psalm 147:3).* Jesus deeply cares about us and asks us to care for others who are walking with us. In John 21:16 Jesus turns to his disciple and directs him to *"Take care of my sheep."* Jesus healed many but involves us by the power of the Spirit to care for others.

David Benner in his book *Soul Care (Page 21)* makes this distinction between care and cure: *"Care* refers to actions that are designed to support the well-being of something or someone. *Cure* refers to actions that are designed to restore well-being that has been lost." They are interrelated as concepts focusing on the well-being of those who travel the pathway of life. Do I care as a neighbor to fellow travelers or can I ignore them thinking I have more important business than the. unfortunate? I don't like my response or lack of response very well.

Q. What are signs of genuine caring to you?

The Pit

(by Marc Fry)

PSALM 40 IS A CRY FOR DELIVERANCE. I LOVE THE DESCRIPTIVE words and desperate emotion expressed by David in this Psalm. It so often seems the times we are most desperate for God is when there is little hope, or we are in a situation where we cannot make it through the circumstances by ourselves.

Contrary to societal beliefs, there is power is surrendering. There is power in being humble and acknowledging our inability to make it on our own. There comes a time in our lives where we need to cry out to God. In Psalm 40, David doesn't just cry out for help and deliverance; he acknowledges the power of God and emphasizes his works and character.

When I think of a pit, I think of something that is very unpleasant, deep, dark, and very difficult to get out of. The brothers of Joseph threw him into an empty well or a deep pit and left him there to die. He was saved but only to be sold into slavery, falsely accused of adultery, and thrown into prison. That's a pretty deep pit.

In the second verse of chapter 40 it says, "He brought me up from the pit, out of the miry clay, and set my feet on a rock and established my steps." The pit makes me think about a difficult situation a person might be in. When one is unable to get out of trouble. The walls or circumstances are so high, there is no way out. You're alone, it's dark. The ground beneath you grabs your legs and feet. There is a feeling of hopelessness and vulnerability.

The pit can often be caused by self-affliction. It can be something we created or got ourselves into. It could be an addiction, it could be trouble with the law, it could be a moral issue or a financial crisis. Other times the pit, as in David's situation, is when evil pursues you and your life. Perhaps your character has come into question, and you are being wrongly accused of something you never did. You've been abused, manipulated or placed into a situation you didn't ask for or even think you would be in. Perhaps it is an illness or financial crisis. These types of pits can be crippling.

I know in my life I have been delivered from the pit. The deepest, most dark, and dangerous pit I've been in were circumstances from self-affliction. God has delivered me from the pit multiple times, but I have also found myself returning to the pit on my own. It is during these times that self-worth is extremely low, depression thrives, and hope begins to fade because a person cannot overcome the lifestyle on their own (the harmful behavior patterns).

Thank God for his grace. We can call out to him because he is our father. Our father loves us and will come when we cry out to him. He will lift us up and out of the pit and put our feet on solid ground. He will go further and even direct our steps. However, it is up to us to be obedient. Consequences from our actions will always follow because just like a father, discipline is involved. A father who does not discipline his child never truly displays true love for his son or daughter.

When we pray, we need to continually humble ourselves and ask God to direct our steps, to protect us from evil, to help us be obedient so we don't find ourselves falling into the pit. Psalm 40 goes on to say that he will put a new song in our mouth and give us a new purpose. I thank God for difficult experiences that help strengthen our faith and cause us to trust in him. I do not, however, want to fall into the pit or return to the pit. There is too much pain, loss and confusion there.

Read Psalm 40

Many Voices

(by Eldon Fry)

EVERY YEAR HUNDREDS EVEN THOUSANDS OF KING PENGUINS gather on the shores of Antarctica.

King penguins breed on sub-Antarctic shorelines of the southern hemisphere where the colony head count can be in tens of thousands or more. Once they couple, the male and female take turns at incubating the egg under their feathers and going fishing to provide the needed nutrients in a harsh context. So how do they manage to find their way back to their partners among the large throng patiently waiting while sitting on eggs? How do young penguins find parents in the chaos of thousands of adult penguins? Dr. Dann, a penguin researcher, explains: "Studies have shown the adults and chicks find each other acoustically. That means penguins call out to each other and rather amazingly can recognize each other's calls among the noise."

Jesus talks to the church in Revelation by saying, *"Here I am! I stand at the door and know, if anyone hears by voice and opens the door, I will come in and eat with him, and he with me."* (3:20). In the Middle East where shepherds still work tending sheep, it is interesting to watch as shepherds call for their sheep to follow them from the common sheepfold. Sheep that we often refer to as "unintelligent" recognize the voice of their shepherd and follow the correct shepherd off to pastures for the day. It is important that they know the voice of their shepherd and not become confused by the voice of many.

Sociologists tell us that we live in a post Christian culture. How do we as followers on the path, sort through the cacophony of voices clamoring for attention and followership? Dallas Willard, former chair of the philosophy department at the University of Southern California and prolific author around spiritual formation, has identified some key aspects of listening in his book, *Hearing God, such as "paying attention to how we hear" (P257)*, a willingness to listen in uneventful moments as well as on demand times, developing practices and habits that create space to hear God, an openness to being surprised by God speaking in ordinary times such as Paul on his way to Tarsus or Moses watching his father-in-law's sheep, avoiding pressure of the demands of perfection or seeking God's will. He states, *"Where God has no instruction to give, we may be sure that is because it is best that he does not. Then whatever lies within is undertaken in faith is his perfect will." (P 269)* Hearing on the journey is dependent on listening well. That is a key to praying along the pathway. How God speaks into our lives as we travel the path may vary greatly but being attentive to the one called the Great Shepherd is key for us to live a life of faith in a community of travelers. We hear God's voice among the many but it is also recognized individually like the acoustic sounds of the King Penguins. Sometimes, it is a verse among the many in the Bible that has been read many times, that suddenly become alive in our minds and spirits to lead us to respond and discover the "green pasture" the Psalmist describes.

Q. When have you been aware of God's voice speaking to your soul?

Eldon E. Fry and Marc A. Fry

Romans Road

(by Marc Fry)

THE ROMAN EMPIRE THRIVED IN THE MIDDLE EAST AND Europe for over 400 years, starting before Christ and ending around 470 A.D. They were brutal in their punishment and treatment of prisoners and people they did not want in society. The Romans did, however, build superior roads during their time of reign. The roads were used primarily for military purposes, enabling them to conquer different lands and manage people. The engineers during that time developed hard surfaces as a foundation that included the use of volcanic ash. Approximately 50,000 miles of hard surface roads were built by the Romans. The roads were known for being straight, flat, and having good drainage. They ran from Spain, throughout the Middle East, and down into parts of Northern Africa. The foundations of the roads were so strong, more modern roads were built on top of them and segments of the original roads are still used today.

(https://www.britannica.com/technology/Roman-road-system)

As we read through the book of Romans, there is a direct route to salvation that has been mapped out by Paul. The "Romans Road" is a solid foundation for one's faith in Jesus Christ. If you have never asked Jesus into your life, this is the path to follow. I have been blessed to use this pathway to lead several people to Christ.

Here are the references that are traditionally used:

Everyone is a sinner. We all need a Savior.

> Romans 3:10 – There is no one who is righteous, not even one.

> Romans 3:23 – For all have sinned and come short of the glory of God.

Sin eventually leads to death.

> Romans 6:23 – For the wages of sin is death, but the gift of God is eternal life through Jesus Christ.

Jesus overcame death to give us life.

> Romans 5:8 – God demonstrated his love for us, in that while we were still sinners, Christ died for us.

We are not condemned if we have a relationship with God.

> Romans 8:1 – There is no condemnation for those who are in Christ Jesus.

If we acknowledge God and ask Jesus into our lives, we become a Child of God.

Romans 10:9 – If you confess with your mouth that Jesus is Lord and believe in your heart that God raised him from the dead, you will be saved.

The road to salvation, and to have a relationship with God is simple. It's not about being good or always doing the right thing. It's about humbling ourselves and accepting Jesus into our lives. Jesus overcame death so we might have eternal life. He has a purpose and plan for us, but the choice is ours.

Here is a simple prayer you can pray out loud to have a relationship with God through Jesus Christ. Once you have a relationship with Jesus you can pray anytime and anyplace. He promises to hear you.

> *Dear God, I believe in you. I believe Jesus died on the cross and rose again. I want to ask you to come into my life. Please forgive me of my sins and my faults. Help me to follow you. Thank you for hearing my prayer. Amen.*

One

(by Eldon Fry)

THE VALUE OF ONE IS OFTEN LOST IN THE MAZE OF INFORMATION and our value depending on "likes" and "friends" in social media. Is there value in touching the life of a single person in a positive way? Jesus seemed to have a way of valuing a person even in the midst of a crowded following. He recognized the touch of a woman on the hem of his garment in the push and shove of a crowd of followers (John 9:20-22). She was healed immediately because of her faith and risk. Jesus identified a short person up in a tree while walking with his followers in Jericho (Luke 19:1-10). Jesus went to the house of Zacchaeus and spent time with this hated tax collector. Jesus summarized by saying, "Today salvation has come to this house...." (:9). There of multiple stories of Jesus valuing the one individual in the midst of a ministry to crowds of followers. Nicodemus came to Jesus by night, ten lepers cried out as he traveled, he met with a woman at the well while his disciples searched for food, he healed the daughter of a leading military man while ministering to the crowd. Each one was a valuable engagement among the many of Israel.

In an age of meg stars and popularity as a key value, Jesus teaches us by example of the value of one. His set of parables in Luke 15 reinforces the value of one. They are stories of one lost sheep and the shepherd leaves 99 safe one for one lost sheep. He and friends celebrate the found and safe lost sheep. "I tell you that in the same way there will be more rejoicing in heaven over one sinner who repents than over ninety-nine righteous person who do not need to repent." (:7) The next story affirms the celebration by the owner and her friends when a lost coin is found and finally the familiar story of the lost son (:11-32) reveals the importance of the return of a son thought to be lost but returns home to the father and a celebration. While we desire a crowd to join us on the sacred path, the one person who joins is to be celebrated and welcomed on the path. The value of the one person makes God very happy indeed and needs to be celebrated.

Jesus stories often involved one person. In Luke 10 the story of the Good Samaritan is used to prioritize our neighbor, the one we have opportunity to serve. The beaten and disregarded man was left by the wayside. One man who was viewed as "less than" the culturally acceptable person took time to care for the fallen man. To this day we refer to him as "the good Samaritan." When Jesus said, "Love your neighbor as yourself." He had used singular terms and spoke to the value of one person doing the right thing for one other person. One is important to God. While we may address societal ills and injustices, we cannot overlook the value of one person in the sight of God.

Each person was viewed by Jesus in a relational perspective and embraced a valuable whether a woman caught in adultery and according to the law was to be killed or a hated tax collector or an ignorant fisherman or shepherds living on the margins of society. Each was to be valued. One is important and to be valued by people of the path.

Q. Can you name one person who is in your life that God is inviting you to value and celebrate?

Your Path

(by Marc Fry)

PERHAPS ONE OF THE MOST DIFFICULT THINGS FOR ME IN MY life has been to confirm what is God's will. There are so many paths and decisions we encounter. Most of our decisions have minimal impact upon ourselves and others, but other decisions will affect not only ourselves but those around us, our relationship with the Lord, our future, our finances, our physical health and so much more.

There were times in my life I wasn't really sure what to do, despite prayer and asking advice from others. In these situations, sometimes the decision was made out of inaction. Other times, I went ahead and made decisions based on what I thought was right. I have learned to ask the Lord for direction and usually he will speak to my heart as to what I should do or what path I should take. Other times when I wasn't sure, I would ask him to close the door if a path was not in line with his will, and more often than not the doors would close.

There definitely have been times I have looked back and thought about as to whether I made the right decision or not, and there have been times I definitely did not make the right decision or I was not patient in my decision making. The beautiful thing is that God gives us a choice. He also will patiently help us through any situations or paths we have wrongly pursued if we acknowledge him.

If you are open to doing whatever God wants you to do, he will lead and provide for you. He will use you despite whatever your faults and failures are. The issues of your past will be used to benefit the Lord and others if you surrender to him. There is victory in surrendering your will, life, desires, and future to God. He will use you in everyday situations and the people you encounter and places he leads you will be a journey. It may just be in your own city or area, or it may be across the sea. You may face language barriers, religions and cultures that are not your own. It might mean filling your house with people who need a family or help. It might mean interacting with people on the streets. It might mean rubbing shoulders with wealthy, influential people in order to soften hearts to be able to help those in need. One thing is for sure, you will never be alone, and you will be busy. Your eyes and ears will be opened. People you have known will be seen in a different light. People you have never met will cross your path. There will be needs. People will need encouragement. People will need a friend. People will need salvation. You will hear and see things you never noticed before. You will be forced to interact and perform tasks you never thought you would be doing.

Jeremiah 29:11 is often quoted to encourage believers. Initially it was said directly to the Israelites who were in captivity in Babylon. "For I know the plans I have for you," declares the Lord, "plans to prosper you, not to harm you. Plans for a hope and future." It still applies to us today because if you are a believer, you are God's child. We deal with captivity in our own lives at times. God wants us to have the freedom to serve him and fulfill his purpose.

Proverbs 3:5-6 is another popular verse many believers quote and memorize. "Trust in the Lord with all your heart and lean not on your own understanding. Acknowledge him in all your ways and he will direct your path." The relevance of this verse is amazing.

God has a plan. All we have to do is trust and acknowledge him, and he will help us fulfill our purpose in life.

Eldon E. Fry and Marc A. Fry

My Story – God's Story

(by Eldon Fry)

"WHAT IS YOUR STORY?" WE ALL HAVE STORIES THAT HAVE shaped us and formed us in a variety of ways, but it is challenging to think that my story may be a God story. Too many have suffered abuse, losses, severe pain, and a variety of other pain filled memories or even current issues. How can my story be God's story? I think I can relate with success, achievements and emotional highs but what about the valleys of life? Where do they fit into God's story.

I grew up in the Bitterroot mountains of Idaho. I now live in the rolling hills of Pennsylvania, but my heart remains focused on the mountains, and I hear them calling in my soul. If the mountains nourish my soul, how do the valleys fit God's narrative for my life? Do valleys simply live in the shadows of mountains so that I cannot see what is ahead or do I find myself fearful of the "valley of the shadow of death" (Psalm 23) cast by the loss of the majesty of the mountains? It is comforting to hear the words of the poet/psalmist (Psalm 23:4 NLT) "Even when I walk through the darkest valley, I will not be afraid for you are close beside me. Your rod and your staff they protect and comfort me."

The Psalmist seems to understand that even in the darkest moments of our lives we are living God's story of us. God is nearby to protect and comfort us. God is living this story with us. The poet/psalmist declares, "I run to hide in you." (Psalm 143:9) in another of how my story even in fearful times intersects with God (Psalm 17:8 NLT) "Hide me in the shadow of your wings." Like a feathered hen or eagle the refuge from my fears is found under the wings of a present and concerned God who is the keeper of our hearts/my heart. An old hymn declares,

> *"Under His wings I am safely abiding Though the night deepens, and tempests are wild, Still I can trust Him, I know He will keep me, He has redeemed me, and I am His child.*
>
> *Under His wings-what a refuge in sorrow! How the heart yearningly turns to His rest! Often when earth has no balm for my healing, there I find comfort and there I am blest."*
>
> *Under His Wings (William O. Cushing, author and Ira D. Sankey, composer)*

Our lives are filled with highs and lows, but as followers of Christ and children of God, we have an identity that remains through the highs and lows of our lifetime. We belong to that family identity. Because of that relationship my story becomes God's story just as my children's lives becomes my story. We are inextricably intertwined. We share stories in common. We are different yet our stories belong to each other and are shared as family members.

I remember watching sporting events and identifying with my son and daughter, as a proud parent, when they did well, and suffering with them through the pain of losses. This is a reflection of our lives beyond sports. Win or lose their story is my story. Thank God he has that identity with me.

Printed in the United States
by Baker & Taylor Publisher Services